Problems in

Climate Change

Table of Contents

Introduction

Climate change is already beginning to transform life on Earth. Around the globe, seasons are shifting, temperatures are climbing and sea levels are rising. And meanwhile, our planet must still supply us – and all living things – with air, water, food and safe places to live. If we don't act now, climate change will rapidly alter the lands and waters we all depend upon for survival, leaving our children and grandchildren with a very different world.

Some of the most dangerous consequences of climate change are listed here in this book.

Rising Temperatures

The first problems in climate change are the rising temperatures which cause the Polar Ice Caps to melt little by little. When the Polar Ice Caps melt it cause sea level growth and it can flood land throughout

the area of the coasts.
Further from the ice caps
some land goes into major
drought which means loss
of water that is much
needed in many lands it may
cause some animals to die
even humans. The rise in
temperatures cause many
illness's and can cause a
large amounts of disease

some are easy to cure many are not. The rise in temperatures cause increased storm intensity. The planets oceans are warming, which is causing dangerous consequences such as coral bleaching and rising seas. Many people get heat stroke. A one degree increase may be found in one place, a 12 degree increase in another and many other areas become much colder. In the 20 century the earth's average temperature rose from one degree to its highest level in the past 4 centuries. It's believed the quickest rise in a thousand years. Heat trapping gases given off by

power plants, cars,
deforestation and other
sources are warming up the
planet.

Climate Change

And Impact

Rising Temperatures and changing patterns in rain and other moist stuff are forcing tree and plants round to move toward Polar Regions and up mountain slopes. These vegetation shifts will undermine much of the work and conservation accomplished to date; with the potential to permanently change the conservancy preserves local land trusts even are national parks. In the tundra, thawing permafrost will allow shrubs and trees to grow. In the great plains of the U.S grasslands are most likely to become forests New England's fiery fall foliage will fade as maple and beech forests and go to cooler temperatures.

Climate change and economy

In southern New England, lobster catches have decreased because heat stresses and parasite threats due to sea level rise. This makes those people not make any money and cause hunger.

Climate change is affecting businesses and economies at home and around the world. If action is not taken to curb global carbon emissions, climate change could cost between 5 and 20 percent of the annual global gross domestic product, according to a British Government Report. In comparison, it would take 1 percent of GDP (Gross Domestic Product) to lessen the most damaging effects of climate change, the report says.

Storm Problems

Scientific research indicates that climate change will cause hurricanes and tropical storms to become more intense — lasting longer, unleashing stronger winds, and causing more damage to coastal ecosystems and communities.

Scientists point to higher ocean temperatures the main culprit, since hurricanes and tropical storms get their energy from warm water. As sea surface temperatures rise, developing storms will contain more energy.

At the same time, other factors such as rising sea levels, wetlands disappearing, and increased coastal development threaten to intensify the damage caused by hurricanes and tropical storms.

Acknowledgements

I would like to give thanks to my family and friends, especially my classmates; they have inspired me to write books. I would also like to give another hands up to my teacher, she is the one who taught me! So huge thanks to everyone!

Notes

Notes

www.ingramcontent.com/pod-product-compliance
Lightning Source LLC
Chambersburg PA
CBHW072016280526
45788CB00005B/2071